I0549013

Peeking
At The World Over
Foster Grant's
At Night

by
Gail Rutherford

cover art and design
C Spencer Morris

photographs
Charles Massey
Gail Rutherford

ORIGINAL DEDICATION

TO MY PARENTS
FOR SHOWING ME THE DOOR

TO CHRISTY BINEGER (NOW DECEASED)

FOR OPENING IT
TO BECKY HENDERSON (NOW STERLING)
FRANK EFFLAND
MARY GWIN
CYNDY STAHL (NOW DECEASED)
FOR HOLDING IT
AND TO ME
FOR WALKING THROUGH

CURRENT AND ADDITIONAL DEDICATION

TO LINDA LOWE
FOR KEEPING MY ORIGINAL MANUSCRIPT
FOR 40 PLUS YEARS (THE ONLY COPY LEFT)

TO CAROL SPENCER MORRIS
CLARENCE DEAN BONNER
FOR MAKING THIS BOOK POSSIBLE

AND TO PAMELA P. DAVIS
FOR EVERYTHING THAT IS
MY CURRENT LIFE

Yeah!
Linda

Gail —
So Glad
To have found
This & to Know
it has a good
Home here at
Texas State
university with
all the
Archives
♡

WRITING WORDS

        ON PAPER

TRYING TO LET OTHERS

        KNOW

HOW
I
THINK
FEEL

SPIRITUALLY
INTELLECTUALLY
BUT
MOSTLY
EMOTIONALLY

FOR BY READING
MY WORDS
YOU READ MY THOUGHTS

YOU WILL KNOW MY
STRENGTHS
WEAKNESSES

SO HERE I AM
OPEN TO YOU
HOPEFULLY
YOU WILL NOT

TAKE ADVANTAGE

HELLO I'D LIKE YOU TO MEET ME

    KNOCK
    KNOCK
    KNOCK

I SOMETIMES WONDER ABOUT ME

I WAS TAUGHT TO PUT OTHER BEFORE SELF
BUT WHEN I DO
I AM ACCUSED
I DON'T RESENT PEOPLE
I RESENT THEIR RESENTMENT

WHEN I DO THE THINGS THEY ASK ME TO DO
     DICTATION
AFTER YOU DO A FAVOR SOME OFTENTIMES FORGET
     I HAVE FAULTS
     WEAKNESSES
AND THEY BECOME ALMOST ANGRY
WHEN THEY SEE THESE FAULTS AND WEAKNESSES
     I SOMETIMES WONDER IF I SHOULD TRY AT ALL

KNOCK
KNOCK
KNOCK

I HAVE FAULTS
I MAKE MISTAKES
BUT I DO CARE ABOUT PEOPLE
I DON'T PROFESS TO CARE ABOUT ALL INDIVIDUALLY
I DON'T KNOW ALL INDIVIDUALLY
     I DO GET MAD
     I DO GET HURT
I TRY TO HIDE SOME OF IT

DEAR READER,

*THANK YOU FOR READING MY BOOK. IF YOU FIND A BLANK PAGE AND
THERE ARE QUITE A FEW, PLEASE FEEL FREE TO WRITE YOUR OWN POEMS,
AND START YOUR OWN BOOK.*

HELLO I'D LIKE YOU TO MEET ME (CONTINUED)

NO ONE IS PERFECT
        AND I SHALL NOT PROFESS TO BE PERFECT

I SHALL STRIVE FOR PERFECTION WITHIN MY OWN STANDARDS
        NOT SOMEONE ELSE'S

SOME ASK ME TO STRIVE TO BE BETTER
        BETTER THAN WHAT
                BETTER THAN MYSELF
                HOW MUCH MUST BE GIVEN

A PEDSTAL MAY DEVELOP
AND I FEAR PEDSTALS
FOR THEY HAVE NO FOUNDATIONS
        AND THE HIGHER THEY GO
        THE EASIER IT IS FOR THEM TO TUMBLE

SO I DON'T EXPECT PERFECTION IN ANYTHING I DO
        EXCEPT FALL OFF PEDSTALS

KEEP ME ON LEVEL GROUND

KNOCK
KNOCK
WHO'S THERE
                JUST ME

                        JUST ME

DEFINITION OF HEDONIST

IT IS THE IDEA THAT EVERY PERSON'S PLEASURE SHOULD FAR SURPASS THEIR AMOUNT OF PAIN.

ETHICAL HEDONISM IS SAID TO HAVE BEEN STARTED BY ARISTIPPUS OF CYRENE, A STUDENT OF SOCRATES.

SOMEONE CALLED ME A NAME

SOMEONE CALLED ME A HEDONIST
CAN YOU IMAGINE
SO WHAT DID I SAY

WHY
THANK YOU
OF COURSE

WHEN I LIVED AT GRIM HOTEL IN 1972 FOR 6 WEEKS THE SIGN WAS LIT FOR THE EVENINGS.
THE ONLY PROBLEM AT THAT TIME THE "E" LIGHTS HAD BURNED OUT AND THE SIGN READ

HOT L
GRIM

HOTEL GRIM TEXARKANA, TEXAS

SHALL I TELL YOU OF THE ONCE GRAND
NOW RUN DOWN HOTEL
I CALL MY RESIDENCE

THE LOBBY WITH THE THIRTY FOOT CEILING
AND IT'S ORNATE PLASTER WORK
        THAT ONCE REIGNED
        OVER THE GOWNED AND JEWELED ELITE
        BUT NOW WHOSE PEELING PAINT RAINS
        ON THE OLD AND TRANSIENT

HOW ABOUT THE NARROW CORRIDORS
        ONCE ECHOING LAUGHTER
        BUT NOW ECHOES THE COUGHES OF OLD AGE

AH YES, THE DECORATIVE BALL ROOMS
        WHERE THE CROWDS GATHERED FOR MERRIMENT
        NOW PADLOCKED AND USED FOR STORAGE OF
        WORN OUT FURNITURE

AND THE STORIES OF THE RESIDENTS
WHO WILL TELL YOU
        "I REMEMBER WHEN THIS WAS THE GRANDEST PLACE
        IN TOWN - OH WE HAD SO MANY GOOD TIMES HERE
        IT WAS SO ELEGANT"

HOW LIKE THE GRIM AND IT'S OCCUPANTS
        ONCE GRAND
        NOW OLD
        ONCE FILLED WITH JOY
        NOW EXISTING
        THE NAME ONCE A JOKE
        NOW A REALITY
        ONCE YOUNG
        NOW OLD
        AND NO ONE CARES

ENOUGH

TRUTH
[TROOTH]

NOUN, PLURAL TRUTHS   [TROOTH Z, TROOTHS] (SHOW IPA)
1. THE TRUE OR ACTUAL STATE OF A MATTER: HE TRIED TO FIND OUT
THE TRUTH.
2. CONFORMITY WITH FACT OR REALITY; VERITY: THE TRUTH OF A
STATEMENT.
3. A VERIFIED OR INDISPUTABLE FACT, PROPOSITION, PRINCIPLE, OR
THE LIKE: MATHEMATICAL TRUTHS.
4. THE STATE OR CHARACTER OF BEING TRUE.
5. ACTUALITY OR ACTUAL EXISTENCE.
6. AN OBVIOUS OR ACCEPTED FACT; TRUISM; PLATITUDE.
7. HONESTY; INTEGRITY; TRUTHFULNESS.

TRUTH
YOU COME TO US IN SO MANY FORMS

       WORDS
            WRITTEN
            SPOKEN
            THOUGHTS

TRUTH YOU ARE ALWAYS THERE
A PART OF US

YET SOMETIMES UNSEEN
       OUR UNSEEN WALL OF PROTECTION
       BLOCKS YOU FROM OUR VISION

OUR DOUBT
       INSECURITY
       THE REASON

SELF TRUTH
THE SEARCH FOR PERFECTION
BYPASSED BY MANY INDIVIDUALS
       WHY
       FEAR
IF ONE'S SEARCH FOR PERFECTION CONTINUES BE PREPARED
TO FACE REJECTION...SCORN AND EVEN THE CRUEL BITING PAIN
OF YOUR PEER'S LAUGHTER...NO PAIN AS DEEP

BUT LET THEIR LAUGHTER FALL ON DEAF EARS
       YOU CAN
       IT IS POSSIBLE
BECAUSE OF YOUR INTELLIGENCE, LOVE, AND UNDERSTANDING
THOSE LAUGHING ARE NOT YOUR PEERS, BEINGS INFERIOR
               TO YOURSELF

YOU DO NOT LAUGH AT OTHERS
YOU SOMETIMES CRY
A TRAIT THAT DENOTES KINDNESS, THAT DENOTES LOVE
FOR ONE THAT LOVES IS
FAR SUPERIOR

ONLY THE INFERIOR DEIGN TO RIDICULE

DISSONANT
DISSIDENCE

WITH HOPE

    FOR THEY
    DESTROY
    APATHY

BURSTING FORTH
WITH
UNRESTRAINED
FURY OF EMOTIONS

PREPOSITIONAL OF CHANGE

TEMPORARY

    MEASURED BY
     MILLISECONDS
OF CONCEPTIONAL TIME

AH LIGHT
REBIRTH

MANY FEEL. . . IT IS CHILDISH
A SHIRKING OF RESPONSIBILITY
TO WANT TO
WRITE
OR PAINT
OR SING
OR BE A MUSICIAN

THEY SAY IT IS CHILDISH UNLESS
OF COURSE YOU ARE A SUCCESS

      IN THEIR EYES
      NOT YOURS

      THEN THEY LIKE TO ASSOCIATE WITH THE
      CHILDREN
      OF THE ARTS
      FOR THEY ARE PATRONS OF THE ARTS

BECAUSE
IT IS SOCIALLY ACCEPTABLE

BUT THE PAIN
AND REJECTION
FROM YOUR
CREATIVE BEGINNING
UNTIL SUCCESS. . . . . . . IN THEIR EYES

IS A PAIN
IN YOUR HEART

      AND THEIR ASS

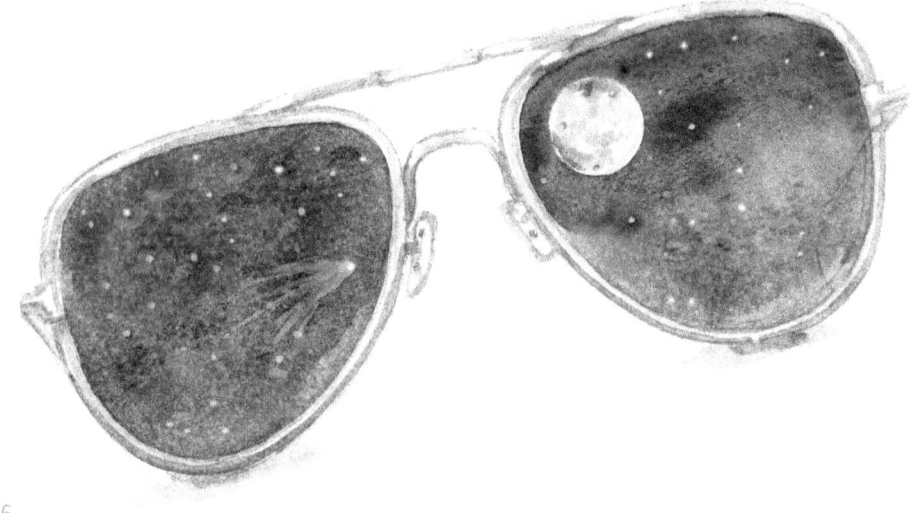

PEEKING

    AT THE WORLD

OVER FOSTER GRANT'S

    AT NIGHT

REVEALS
WHAT IS HIDDEN MOST OF THE TIME

THOSE PEOPLE SLIPPING AROUND
MEETING MORE OF THOSE PEOPLE

THEY CAN
SOMETIMES SPOOK YOU
MAKE YOU FEEL LIKE A KID
    OR FEEL AS THOUGH A SPIKE
    HAS BEEN DRIVEN THROUGH YOUR HEART
OR BE AS SUBTLE AS AN INDIAN
TIPTOEING THRU THE WOODS

ONCE YOU HAVE COLLIDED WITH THOSE PEOPLE
YOUR LIFE WILL BE CHANGED
    A NEW PERSPECTIVE

YOU MAY FEEL IT WOULD BE SAFER TO STAY PROTECTED
BEHIND YOUR FOSTER GRANT'S
IF YOU WANT LIFE
TO REMAIN

    DULL

I MET YOU AT THE LOCAL CARNIVAL
SOME CALL IT A BAR
SOME THINK IT A ZOO
I TEND TO THINK OF IT AS A CARNIVAL

EVERYTHING WAS FREE ... EVEN ME
GRAND OPENING
      PINBALL MACHINES, LIGHTS, BELLS
      CONCENTRATION
      AND A GAME WON

YOU WENT WITH ME TO MEET A FRIEND
BUSINESS TAKEN CARE OF
YOU READ MY POETRY
A REFLECTION OF SELF ... YOU SAY
      EMOTIONALLY

YOU REACHED OUT AND TOUCHED ME
PHYSICALLY, I RESPONDED
WE DID NOT SLEEP
I ASK YOU TO STAY
I COULD SET THE ALARM
YOU SAID OKAY
      I KNEW YOU WOULD NOT STAY
      YOU KNEW YOU WOULD NOT STAY
      BUT YOU DID NOT KNOW I KNEW

YOU ASK QUESTIONS
I ANSWERED SOME
SOME I SAID WERE NONE OF YOUR BUSINESS

YOU ASK IF I WERE AND INTELLECTUAL
I SAID NO.....WHAT IS AN INTELLECTUAL

EVERYONE HAS TO HAVE HOBBIES
YOU WANT TO SEE ME AGAIN
OKAY

      NO I DON'T HAVE A PHONE
      IF IT'S MEANT TO BE

THE SELECT A MATE

THAT LAST CHANCE SALOON

CROWDS GATHERING
AFTER THE MIDNIGHT HOUR

AND THE TALENT ONSTAGE
        AND THE AUDIENCE ON STAGE

SILENTLY PLEADING
        HEY LOOK AT ME

RAMPANT LONELINESS
AND IT'S ALMOST CLOSING TIME
        THE LINES
                THE COME ONS
                THE PUT DOWNS

ALL RIGHT TIME TO CLOSE EVERYBODY GO HOME

SOME READY
        HOPEFUL
        LOVE WILL BLOOM
        FROM THIS UPCOMING
                ONE NIGHT STAND

HOW EASY IT IS
TO CONVINCE ONSELF
        WHEN
                ONE
                        IS
LONELY

SUITS ABOUNDING
EVEN THOSE IN JEANS
          STARCHED
HAVE A SUIT LOOK

THAT OVER THIRTY CROWD

LOOKING FOR LIFE
THEY HAVE MISSED
LAUGHTER SO LOUD
IT SEEMS
          FORCED AND STRAINED
WINKING
PATTING
          EXECUTIVES
          POLITICIANS
                    LOOKING FOR
          FEMALE COMPANY
                    LOOKING FOR
          EXECUTIVES
          POLITICIANS

YOU CAN ALMOST SENSE
THE ALMOST FORGOTTEN
                    FREEDOM OF YOUTH
                    THAT THEY HAVE
                    LOST TOUCH WITH
DUE TO SELF IMPOSED
RESPONSIBILITY

SO THEY SPEND THAT MONEY
SEEK GREATER FORTUNES
AND AS THEY DO
FORGET TOTALLY

THAT FREEDOM OF YOUTH

THAT FREEDOM
TO REACH OUT
AND TOUCH

LOST ON COUNTRY ROADS

BUT KNOWING WE WILL FIND OUR WAY
NO FEAR
        JUST FUN
LAUGHTER

MUSIC
AND THE BUZZ OF THE ENGINE
OF THE FORTY NINE CHEVROLET

OLD BARNS
THAT NEED REST

FIELDS OF ICE AND SNOW

AND A
CRAZY WILD
TURKEY IN THE WAY

TURN HERE
                NO GO STRAIGHT

IT'S LATE
WHERE ARE WE
WHO KNOWS
WE ARE SOMEWHERE

        CAN YOU PICTURE A BALLET
        FEELING SO HIGH
        WE CAN PENETRATE THE SKY

QUESTIONS BEING ASK
ANSWERS BEING FELT
TOTAL PERCEPTION
        OF HAPPINESS
AS A REFLECTION OF MOONSHINE ON SNOW
CREATES HUES OF BLUE ACROSS THE VALLEY

WONDERING HOW SUCH COLD OUTSIDE
CAN CREATE SUCH WARMTH WITHIN
ESTATIC WAVES OF CONTENTMENT

DAYS PASS

AND YOUR SETTING HAUNTS MY SOUL

I WOULD WATCH YOU FADE BEHIND THE MOUNTAINS
AS ALL THE COLORS OF THE RAINBOW

BURST ACROSS
THE SKY

PROCLAIMING YOUR POWER

WAKAN TANKA
SO POETIC

FOR WITHOUT YOU NO LIFE
MERELY FROZEN DESOLATION

YET

THE DESERT A REMINDER OF YOUR POWER

27

SEASONS OF GROWTH

      I WONDER IF
PLANTS
HAVE
GROWING PAINS

CONTEMPLATING MY FUTURE GROWTH
I WANT IT TO BE UPWARD
YET A PUSH TO REACH THE TOP
TOO FAST
MAY LEAD TO
MY FAILURE TO NOTICE
THE SUNSHINE AND IT'S WARM RAYS
AND WITHOUT THOSE LIFE GIVING RAYS
WE LET IN THE SHADOWS OF STAGNATION
IN PERSUIT OF FORGOTTEN DREAMS

TOWARD THAT GOAL OF SUCCESS

SO LET US CONTEMPLATE THE SLOW GROWTH
OF DISCOVERY
LET US GROW TOWARD THE SUN
WITH LIGHT
ILLUMINATING
ALL AROUND US

SO WE WILL BE AWARE OF WHAT IS
PAST
PRESENT
FOR WE ONLY HAVE
MINUTE
CONTROL OVER THE FUTURE

RAINY DAYS

THANK YOU FOR FORCING ME TO STOP
        AND LISTEN TO MY THOUGHTS

I SOMETIMES TEND
TO GO IN EVERY DIRECTION AT ONCE
AND ONLY OCCASIONALLY
        LISTEN TO ME

WHAT'S REALLY NICE
I LIKE WHAT I HEAR

LOVE, WARMTH
        DON'T MISTAKE
        APPRECIATION
        FOR EGOTISM

YES, APPRECIATION
        I APPRECIATE THE FACT I LIKE ME
        I APPRECIATE THE FACT I AM IMPORTANT

I SOMETIMES GET TOO BUSY
TO REMEMBER THAT FACT

IF I DON'T CARE FOR ME
HOW CAN I CARE FOR OTHERS

RAINY DAYS
        SOMETIMES
        YOU ARE MORE WELCOME THAN SUNSHINE

I THINK THIS WEEKEND
I WOULD LIKE TO GO
TO THE WOODS

TO THE WOODS
TO THE WOODS

AND BE WITH NATURE
I WONDER IF I DARE TO DRIVE CLYDE
(MY OLD STATIONWAGON)
PROBABLY NOT OUT OF THE CITY

BUT I CAN ALMOST HEAR THE BUFFAO RIVER
RUSHING ALONG AFTER THE FALL RAINS
THE BREEZE THROUGH THE TREES

      AND THE SUN PEEKING THROUGH THE LEAVES
          AND BRANCHES

           SAYING

HERE I AM
WATCH MY LIGHT DIFFUSE

AND AS I LOOK UP

THE LIGHT WILL CATCH ME PEEKING
AND I'LL SQUINT
SO I CAN SEE THE LIGHT
     DANCING FROM LEAF TO LEAF
     AND BRANCH TO BRANCH

AND I'LL SHOUT
JUBILATION

FREEDOM
BEAUTY
AND LIFE

FORGOTTEN FOOTSTEPS

ECHO
ACROSS
THE BAREN FIELDS

      AS YESTERDAY'S DREAMERS
      SEARCH
      FOR THEIR TOMORROWS
      IN A NEW
   UNPOPULATED LAND
   WITH HOPE ACTING AS THEIR STIMULUS

I WONDER
IF
WE
ARE THE ANSWER TO THEIR DREAMS
OR MERELY
A NIGHTMARE COME TRUE

      IS THIS THE TYPE OF LIFE THEY INVISIONED
      THE TYPE OF LIFE THEY WERE SEEKING
      OR THE TYPE OF LIFE
      THEY WERE SEEKING TO ESCAPE

FOR IT SEEMS TODAY
I
SEARCH
FOR MY TOMORROWS

      WITH HOPE
      OF FRIENDSHIP AND LOVE
      ACTING AS MY STIMULUS

THE SOFT
PASTEL SUNSET

OVER THE SNOW COVERED BOTTOM LAND

AND

        A

            LONE TREE

WITH A CAR PARKED
BENEATH
IT'S AGE WEARY BRANCHES

AN OLD BRIDGE
COVERED WITH ICE

AND THOSE FANTASTIC COLORS

STOP
WHEN YOU TURN RIGHT

WHAT
      YOU'LL SEE

THE SUNSET
ROADS UNPAVED
      WITH ICY RUTS

AND ALL OF US

WATCHING THE SUN RISE
HAVE YOU SEEN IT

WATCHING THE SKY CHANGE
DO YOU REALLY FEEL IT

HOW CAN ONE BE CONTENT
MISSING THE SUNRISE

      WE SAT AND TALKED
      I LISTENED TO YOU SING
      I HEARD AND WATCHED YOU PLAY

YOU PUT YOUR HEART OUT
I COULD SEE IT BLEEDING

EVERYTHING IS GOING FINE, SO YOU SAY
BUT ALL THE MEMORIES
STILL CAUSE PAIN

YOU'RE GOING TO BE ON TOP SOMEDAY

      SOMEDAY
      SOMEDAY

AS LONG AS YOU KEEP GROWING

      I HAVE A LOT OF FRIENDS
      I SIT AND LISTEN TO THEM SING
      I HEAR AND WATCH THEM PLAY

THEY PUT THEIR HEARTS OUT
I CAN SEEM THEM BLEEDING

NOW, EVERYTHING IS GOING TO FINE, SO THEY SAY
THEY'RE GOING TO BE ON TOP SOMEDAY

BUT THE PAIN JUST WON'T GO AWAY

SO MANY VIBES BOUNCING
AROUND AT ONCE

CYNDY WAS BACK FROM EUROPE
AND YOUR SOUL WAS SMILING
      LOWE
        YOUR HAPPINESS
        RADIATED
        THE ROOM
        SAME FOR HER

SHE BROUGHT HER FRIEND DAN
YOU BROUGHT YOUR FRIENDS

YOU SANG YOUR SONGS TO ONE ANOTHER
AND WARMTH ENCOMPASSED THE ROOM
        AND THE SOULS THEREIN

AND MY SOUL
WAS SMILING
MUTUAL ADMIRATION
        FRIENDSHIP AND LOVE

THANK YOU MY SISTERS AND BROTHERS
OF MY UNIVERSE
SO SELDOM
        THIS HAPPINESS

WHY DO SO MANY FAIL TO SMILE
AT ONE ANOTHER

        THANK YOU
        FOR BEING MY FRIENDS

BUT SOMETIMES
WHEN WE THINK
WE ARE NOT ALWAYS CORRECT

COMPLICATED LADY
CONTRADICTORY LADY
BUT I GUESS CONTRADICTION
IS ALL A PART OF COMPLEXITY

YOU ARE SO ALOOF
ALMOST COCKY
        ALMOST
        TO MANY YOU ARE

YET I KNOW YOUR SENSITIVITY
        WHEN YOU SLAM A DOOR
        HANG UP THE PHONE
        DON'T SPEAK
SOME WILL NOT UNDERSTAND
BUT YOU MUST NOT FORGET
THERE ARE OTHERS IN THIS WORLD JUST AS SENSITIVE

YOU
HAVE TO INITIATE
ACTION
RATHER THAN REACT TO THEIR NON ACTION

YOU NEVER LET GO OF YOUR LOVES
EVEN LOST LOVES
BUT DON'T LET THEIR GHOSTS PREVENT
NEW LOVES
DON'T LET HURT PREVENT GROWTH

GROWTH
WHICH IS AN ERADICATOR OF HURT

HOW DECEIVING
YOUR FRAGILE STRENGTH
YOU ARE STRONGER THAN YOU THINK
BUT NOT AS STRONG AS SOME THINK
        YOU NEED A SHOULDER TO CRY ON
        FOR YOUR TEARS FLOW OFTEN
MANY TIMES FOR THOSE THAT ARE NOT AWARE
YOU CANNOT HIDE YOUR EMOTIONS
        WHICH MAKES YOU VULNERABLE
        TO LESS SENSITIVE

SUCH A WONDERFUL VISIT

SO NICE TO FIND

SOUL GROWTH PATTERNS SIMILIAR
TO MY OWN

HOW NICE
SOME
HAVE FOUND
THE WISDOM OF SENSITIVITY

WHILE STROKING THROUGH
THOSE BUSINESS YEARS

SO NOW I WILL LEAVE
KNOWING

I HAVE A PLACE
TO RETURN TO

IN
THE
FUTURE

THE JOY OF LOVE

BOUNCING OFF PLASTIC WALLS
MELTING
FANTASY

AND CREATING A WARM REALITY
CHILDREN LAUGHING
AND TOUCHING YOUR HAND
      REACHING OUT

WHILE THE MUSIC PENETRATES OUR SOULS
STRANGERS BONDED NO LONGER STRANGERS

ELEPHANTS WATCHING
THE SYMBOL UNKNOWN EXCEPT TO THOSE WHO KNOW
OF THE WISDOM OF IT'S MISTRESS
THE SONGSTRESS

AND YOUR OFF THE WALL BLUES
OFF KEY
PROOF AGAIN THAT LOVE
BRINGS LOVE
      (YOU LAUGHING AS YOU ASK...WAS THAT OFF KEY)

THANK YOU THOSE YOU HAVE NEVER MET BEFORE

TO LOVE AND SHARE
WITH THOSE YOU HAVE NEVER MET BEFORE

FOR THROUGH YOU AND YOUR WARMTH
AND YOU AND YOUR FRIENDS
ALL THAT ARE TOUCHED BY YOU
BECOME THOSE THAT KNOW

YOU PASSED HIM BY
TEARS
ROLLING DOWN YOUR CHEEKS
THE PAIN YOU FEEL
EVIDENT
TO ALL

WHO KNEW
FIVE YEARS IS A LONG TIME
OH MARRIED MEN
IS IT A GAME
IS IT LOVE
IT IS A LACK OF COURAGE

ALL OF US KNOW
HOW MUCH YOU LOVE HIM
ALL YOUR FRIENDS

ALL OF HIS FRIENDS
SAY HE LOVES YOU
HE IS A MAN OF HIS WORD

HE MADE HIS CHOICE
NO MATTER THE REASONS
THAT DOES NOT EASE YOUR PAIN

HAVE A KLEENEX
THAT'S ALL I CAN DO
I CAN'T EASE YOUR PAIN
HOW HELPLESS
          WE ALL ARE
HOW HELPLESS YOU ARE
WHEN HE IS NEAR

PAIN IS NOT ALWAYS THE SAME
BUT IT ALWAYS HURTS

MAYBE ONE DAY
YOUR LOVE FOR HIM WILL FADE
AND YOU WILL NOT CRY
WHEN YOU PASS HIM BY

SEARCHING
SEARCHING
SEARCHING
        MY FRIEND
WATCHING OVER THE HILLS OF MISSOURI
YOU PUT YOURSELF THROUGH SO MANY CHANGES
OTHERS PUT YOU THROUGH SO MANY CHANGES
        YOU ARE A STRANGER STRIDING
        SEEKING A GOAL
I HAVE NEVER HEARD A DEROGATORY WORD
PASS BETWEEN YOUR LIPS
        EVEN FOR THOSE WHO HAVE CAUSED YOU GREAT PHYSICAL
        AND MENTAL PAIN
                DEGRADATION
YOU BLAME SELF
NOT THOSE STRANGERS IN THE NIGHT
THE PEOPLE OF DARKNESS
WITH SHADOWS FOR A SOUL
WHY WON'T SOMEONE HELP YOU ACROSS THE BRIDGE
        FOR THEY ARE IN AWE OF YOU
        AND YOU CAN'T UNDERSTAND WHY
        THEY WOULD LIKE TO LIVE AS A MILLIONAIRE
                YOU HAVE
        THEY WOULD LIKE TO SING BEFORE AN AUDIENCE AND HEAR APPLAUSE
                YOU HAVE
        THEY WOULD LIKE TO WRITE A SONG
                YOU HAVE
        THEY WOULD LIKE TO WRITE A CHILDREN'S STORY
                YOU HAVE
        THEY WOULD LIKE TO TRAVEL ACROSS THE COUNTRY
                YOU HAVE
        THEY WOULD LIKE TO "BUM" AROUND EUROPE
                YOU HAVE
        THEY WOULD LIKE TO HAVE A KNIGHT IN SHINING ARMOR TO LOVE
                YOU HAVE
        THEY WOULD LIKE TO GET HIGH
                YOU HAVE
        THEY WOULD LIKE TO PAINT A PICTURE
                YOU HAVE
        THEY WOULD LIKE TO CALL ARTISTS, WRITERS, MUSICIANS "FRIEND"
                YOU HAVE

SEARCHING (CONTINUED)

THEY DREAD LOSING SOMEONE THEY LOVE
      YOU HAVE
THEY FEAR NOT HAVING A HOME
      YOU HAVE
THEY FEAR BEING RAPED PHYSICALLY
      YOU HAVE
THEY FEAR BEING RAPED MENTALLY
      YOU HAVE
THEY WONDER WHAT PEGGY LEE MEANT WHEN SHE SANG
      "IS THAT ALL THERE IS"
          YOU KNOW
THEY WONDER WHAT IT WOULD TAKE TO MAKE THEM LOVE LIFE
      YOU'RE LOOKING

YOU KNOW FEAR
AND NOW YOU FEAR FEAR

REMEMBER THE WISE WORDS OF A PASSING STRANGER
WHO IS INGRAINED IN YOUR MEMORY......HEART

YOU WONDER WHY THEY SIT AND LISTEN
THEY CAN FEEL THEIR PAIN WITH YOU
THEY CAN FEEL THEIR LOVE WITH YOU
YOU TELL THEM WHO THEY ARE
HOW SO MANY OTHERS SEE THEM

WHO THEY REALLY ARE
YOU SING THE SONG YOU HAVE WRITTEN JUST FOR THEM

THEY FEEL LOVE
SOMEONE
SOMEONE

LOVES ENOUGH
TO WRITE SOME WORDS
TO TELL THE WORLD WHO THEY REALLY REALLY ARE

THEY PAY HOMAGE TO YOU
OF COURSE

YOU PAY HOMAGE TO THEM
WITH YOUR WORDS

THEY'LL APPLAUD FOR YOU
THEY'LL FEEL WITH YOU

YOU SHOW THEM LOVE
A LOVE THEY HAVE NEVER KNOWN BEFORE
THEY KNOW NUMEROUS PEOPLE
BUT NO ONE HAS EVER CARED ENOUGH
TO TELL THE WORLD ABOUT THEM

TO TELL THE WORLD WHO THEY REALLY ARE

GAIL RUTHERFORD

A NEW FRIEND
I REALLY DON'T KNOW YOU
BUT YOU ARE A FRIEND

      A STRANGE STATEMENT
      UNUSUAL ANYWAY
      FOR ME

I KNOW MANY WELL
BUT THAT DOES NOT MAKE THEM FRIENDS

I KNOW SOME
THAT DON'T KNOW YOU
YET HAVE FORMED THE OPINION
THEY DON'T WANT TO

YET OTHERS WANT TO BE NEAR YOU
BUT DON'T WANT TO KNOW YOU

I SEE THE GLINT IN YOUR EYE

      FOR THEY WILL NEVER KNOW
      YOUR INTELLIGENCE
      FOR THEY HAVE NEVER SEEN
      YOUR SOUL

AND THEY DON'T RECOGNIZE THE FACT
YOU KNOW

YOU HAVE FUN
LAUGHING AT THE CLOWNS
ONE CAN'T HELP
BUT
LAUGH AT CLOWNS

I DO
MAYBE
THAT'S THE REASON
FOR OUR
      MUTUAL RECOGNITION

HOW OSTENTATIOUS YOU ARE

ARE YOU EVER OFF STAGE
ARE YOU AFRAID NOT TO PERFORM
        DO YOU KNOW HOW YOU USE OTHERS
ARE YOU AWARE
        DO YOU CARE

YOU ARE PITIABLE

YOU WONDER WHY PEOPLE
BECOME A PART OF YOUR LIFE
THEN TAKE THE NEAREST EXIT

        BECAUSE THEY HAVE TO BRING
        THE CURTAIN DOWN
        SINCE YOU WON'T

I WANTED TO CALL YOU FRIEND
BUT YOUR FRIENDS ARE MAKE BELIEVE
YOU MAKE BELIEVE
THEY MAKE BELIEVE

AND AFTER THE SHOW CLOSES
THEY KEEP ON LAUGHING
HOW SAD IT WAS A DRAMA

        SO WHY DO I STILL BUY TICKETS

WHEN YOU SING YOUR SONG

HOW MANY LISTEN TO THE WORDS

OR BETTER YET HOW MANY FEEL YOUR WORDS
YOU DO

      SO
      SO
      SO

FOR ME
FOR ME IT IS EVIDENT

DOES ALL THAT ALCOHOL THEY ARE
CONSUMING
DULL THEIR SENSES SO COMPLETELY

      OR WERE THEY DULLED BEFORE

IT SEEMS LIKE A LIFETIME

BUT ONLY A FEW WEEKS HAVE PASSED
WHEN ALL OF US WERE TOGETHER

YOU CAME BACK FOR A BRIEF VISIT
BUT THE PRESENCE OF OTHERS
STILL AWAY
WAS MISSED

NEW SONGS

YOU ASK HOW I LIKE THEM
WHAT CAN I SAY

THEY BROUGHT ME PEACE
A PEACE I HAVE MISSED
        LOWE THESE PAST FEW WEEKS

YOUR MUSIC
        YOUR WORDS

PARENTAL PERSONS
I WONDER IF WE'LL ALWAYS BE CHILDREN
        WE SEEM ADULT
        WE LOOK ADULT
        TO OURSELVES
        OUR PEERS
                    BUT

WE'RE ALWAYS THE KIDS
TO THOSE PARENTAL PERSONS
        AND WE WONDER AS ADULTS
        WHY THEY TREAT US AS CHILDREN
        AND THEY WONDER WHY THEIR CHILDREN
        DON'T ACT AS ADULTS
AND THEY WANT US TO MAKE IT ON OUR OWN
AS THEY DAYDREAM OF ROCKING US
AS THEY DAYDREAM OF CHANGING OUR DIAPERS
        BUT HOW NICE IT IS
        WHEN AS AN ADULT
        YOU HURT AS A CHILD
        AND THEY
        MERELY BY SIGHT SOOTH AWAY PART OF THE PAIN
        WITH THE SECURITY OF THEIR BEING

AND THEY WANT US TO BE ADULTS
AND LIVE ON OUR OWN

AS THEY DAYDREAM OF THE DAY WE WERE BORN
AS THEY DAYDREAM OF OUR FIFTH BIRTHDAY

AND THEY WONDER WHY THEIR CHILDREN
DON'T ACT AS ADULTS
ALL THE WHILE ACTING AS PARENTAL PERSONS

KNOWING THE RELIEF
THEY GIVE US
KNOWING WE WILL GO AWAY AGAIN
TILL NEXT VACATION
TILL NEXT TIME
        DO THEY KNOW WE KNOW THEY KNOW

The Linda Lowe
Songbook

All my best

Even the moon

So far apart

Lucid dreamer

Little by Little

Gamblin with the wind

Out here in the crossing

The Rollin Records Collection

HOW DID IT FEEL TO HAVE

THE SPOTLIGHT ON YOU

HOW DID IT FEEL
NOT
TO BE ON THE DEFENSIVE

I THINK I KNOW

      I CAN FEEL YOUR SMILE
      SMILING OVER THE PHONE

APPLAUSE
APPLAUSE

HOW DID IT FEEL TO KNOW
THEY WERE LISTENING
TO EVERY NOTE

AND THEN
      SILENCE
AND THEN

      APPLAUSE
      APPLAUSE
      APPLAUSE

BRRRR
COLD
AND I DIDN'T WANT TO DROP MY CAMERA
IN THE WATER
THE ROCKS WERE SLIPPERY

COLD
WADING BAREFOOTED
THE CHILL STINGING
THE JOY OF LIFE
NO LONGER IN A STATE OF MERE EXISTANCE

      EUPHORIA

I LIKE RAPID FLOWING CREEKS
I ONCE SAW A RIVER NO LARGER THAN THIS CREEK
      RELATIVITY

THE MOON IS SHINING OPPOSITE
THE SETTING SUN
      PEACE

PEACE
ONLY DISTURBED BY THE GURGLING OF WATER
OVER ROCKS

      CONTENTMENT

THEN MY FRIEND
LAUGHING
RUNNING ALONG THE CREEK BANK MAKING CRAZY FACES
      PEACE
      CONTENTMENT
REPLACED WITH LAUGHTER
AND CRAZY ANTICS

WHAT MORE COULD ONE ASK FOR IN A SINGLE DAY
SOME NEVER HAVE THIS
OR AT LEAST NEVER RECOGNIZE THIS

      EVEN IN A LIFETIME

THE FOLLOWING POEM WAS WRITTEN
ABOUT A FRIEND WHO WAS BEING
BULLIED.

WHEN I WASN'T LOOKING I ALMOST LOST A FRIEND

YOU THOUGHT YOU WERE ALONE
NEVER
ALL YOU HAD TO DO WAS SAY
HEY I'M OVER HERE
MANY TIMES WE FAIL TO SEE THE PROBLEMS OF OTHERS

MY PROBLEMS HAVE NEVER BEEN SO COMPLICATED
THAT I WOULD CONTEMPLATE SELF INFLICTED DEATH
MANY TIMES WE HAVE PROBLEMS OF OUR OWN
        HOW SIMPLE MY OWN LIFE
        MY OWN PROBLEMS
BUT YOURS
SO MAGNFIED BY LONELINESS, RUMORS, AND GOSSIP
        YOU WANTED TO TAKE YOUR OWN LIFE

I GUESS MANY THINK ABOUT OR THREATEN SUICIDE
        BUT TO ATTEMPT IT AND ALMOST SUCCEED
                IN STOPPING YOUR OWN VITAL SIGNS
TO MOST IT IS ONLY A FLEETING THOUGHT

MY DEAR DEAR FRIEND
I AM SORRY YOU FELT SO ALONE IN THIS WORLD
        RUMOR MONGERS
        REMEMBER ONLY YOU KNOW THE TRUTH
        NOT PASSING ACQUAINTANCES
        CERTAINLY NOT STRANGERS
YOU ALONE KNOW THE TRUTH OF YOU
AND THROUGH YOU THOSE THAT CARE

NO ONE ELSE MATTERS
THOSE THAT TURN AWAY WERE NEVER YOUR FRIENDS
        MERELY POWER SEEKERS
        THAT WANTED TO DICTATE YOUR LIFE
        BY THEIR STANDARDS
NOT SUPPORT YOU
IN YOUR GROWTH
YOUR TRUE FRIENDS ARE HERE NOW

YOU WERE
BUT NOW NO LONGER
YOUR SMILE
ERASED
NON EXISTANT

YOUR LAUGHTER
GONE

WE MISS YOU
I'M GLAD I'M NOT THERE
TO VIEW YOUR DEATH DAILY

SO I WILL SAY GOODBYE
NOW

FOR YOU ARE GONE
ONLY A LIFELESS SHELL

AND
NO ONE
WILL
PULL THE PLUG

I KNOW YOU

LOCAL TALENT

THAT WILL NEVER MAKE IT

TO WHERE
YOU ASK

ANYWHERE BUT WHERE YOU ARE

BECAUSE YOU DO NOT LISTEN
YOU ARE CLOSED

      YOU THINK YOU'RE REALLY
GOOD

BUT YOU DON'T KNOW IT
AND THAT'S
      THE DIFFERENCE

SOME THINGS COME AND GO
SOME THINGS HAVE A BEGINNING AND END
BUT THE THREE RING CIRCUS NEVER ENDS
HOW SAD YOU ARE
      THE CLOWN
WITH A SMILE PAINTED ON YOUR FACE
      BUT WITH A FROWN EVER PRESENT BENEATH
SOMETIMES YOU DON'T EVEN KNOW IT'S THERE
A MOMENT OF LAUGHTER
HOW HOLLOW
      BUT YOU NEVER HEAR THE ECHO
ALL THOSE AROUND YOU
THE PERFORMERS
LAUGHING....CRYING
      I LEFT THE CIRCUS
BUT I AM STILL TOUCHED
      AND NOT TENDERLY
BY THE TRICKS THEREIN
      I HAVE NEVER LIED
      ABOUT THE CIRCUS
      ONLY THE TRUTH HAS PASSED BETWEEN MY LIPS
WHERE WILL YOU BE WHEN THE RINGMASTER
HAS TIRED OF YOUR TRICKS
OTHER ACTS HAVE BEEN HIRED THEN FIRED
THE CIRCUS WORLD IS ALL YOU KNOW NOW
      WHAT OF REAL PEOPLE
      THE REAL WORLD
HOW CAN YOU COPE
SILLY CLOWN...WITHOUT ALL THE CIRCUS PUPPETS

NOW I UNDERSTAND WHY THE SMILE IS PAINTED ON

THE CIRCUS WORLD
ILLUSIONS....MAKE BELIEVE

WHAT IS TRUTH
WHERE WILL YOU FIND IT
      WHEN WILL YOU FIND IT

I KNOW SOMEONE THAT WENT TO EUROPE
AND COMMENTED

> EVERYTHING THERE IS OLD

LOOKING AT THE PAST THROUGH THE EYES
OF SOMEONE THAT DOES NOT HAVE THE SOUL OF AN ARTIST

LOOKING AT THE PAST
        TALKING

AND NOT FEEL WHAT YOUR EYES BEHELD

THERE THE PAST THAT COULD SHOW YOU THE FUTURE
AND NOT RECOGNIZE

        TO TOUCH THE MARBLE THE ARTIST
        SCULPTED
        WITH LOVE
        WITH JOY
        WITH PAIN
AND NOT BE IN AWE

DREAMS DIFFER
AS PEOPLE

TO KNOW SOMEONE THAT LIVED MY DREAM
AND DIDN'T WAKE
        TO APPRECIATE THE PRIVILIGE
        OF EXPERIENCING

I THINK

THE DEFENSE MECHANISMS
OF THE WORLD
         OF PEOPLE
ARE
FUNNY
STRANGE

MOST THINK THEY CAN HIDE THEIR
WALLS

        WALLS EVERYWHERE
        AROUND PEOPLE
        AROUND GOVERNMENTS

FUNNY
BUT THOSE WITH X-RAY VISION

        GET ALL THE LAUGHS

SEEK AND YE SHALL FIND

BUT BEFORE YOU CAN FIND
YOU MUST KNOW WHAT YOU ARE SEEKING
        I SEEK LIFE

BUT WHICH FACET
THERE ARE SO MANY
AND SO MANY STEPS TO TAKE

AND THE TIME IS SO SHORT
        AT LEAST TIME AS WE KNOW IT TO BE

THERE ARE MANY IN THIS WORLD CONTENT
AND I AM ENVIOUS OF THEIR CONTENTMENT
YET
THEY TELL ME THEY ARE ENVIOUS OF MY FREEDOM

        MY FREEDOM

MY CUROSITY
I ALWAYS QUESTION
        EVEN MY OWN SEEKING
I DO LEARN

YET I HAVE NOT LEARNED WHAT I SEEK
        ABOUT LIFE

BUT WHEN I LEARN
I WILL THEN KNOW
        DEATH

YOU DON'T WANT WHAT I HAVE TO OFFER

YOU DON'T KNOW WHAT I HAVE
YOU ALMOST FOUND OUT

BUT YOU WERE BLINDED

YOU THINK YOU KNOW WHAT YOU WANT

YOU THINK
YOU KNOW

AND HOW COULD YOU BE WRONG

AND WHEN I'M GONE

YOU WILL STILL
NOT KNOW

FOR THE BLIND CANNOT SEE
AND YOU'LL NEVER KNOW ME

I'M GONE

AREN'T OLD FASHIONED VALENTINES SWEET

SO YOU KNOW

BUT DO YOU KNOW
        HOW I LOVE YOU

DO YOU CARE
        HOW I NEED YOU

CAN WE
JUST A LITTLE TIME
IS IT POSSIBLE FOR US TO SHARE

WILL YOU BE MINE
        NOT A POSSESSION

BUT A PART
        FOR NOT REALIZING
YOU HAVE MY HEART

YOU MAY LEAVE

BUT DON'T LEAVE
        WITHOUT GIVING ME TIME
FOR YOU
TO KNOW
TO CARE
TO SHARE

SO LITTLE
I THINK I ASK

        BUT IF YOU ASK ME THE SAME
        I MIGHT FEEL YOU SELFISH

DID YOU "HEAR"

YOU KNOW "WHAT I HEARD"
WERE YOU "TOLD"

LET ME "TELL YOU"

ALL THOSE WORDS OR PHRASES
ARE USUALLY FOLLOWED BY
        A DERAGATORY REMARK
        OR GOSSIP

GOSSIP
WHICH IS USUALLY NINTY PERCENT
        PEPPERED WITH IMAGINATION
        OR WORSE YET LIES
AND SPRINKLED WITH TEN PERCENT
        TRUTH

HAVE YOU EVER

      HAD THE THOUGHT

"I HAD THIS THOUGHT"

AND NOW IT'S GONE
AND THE RECALL
BUTTON

ON YOUR MEMORY BANK
IS NOT WORKING

WORDS
THOUGHTS
THEY COME
THEY GO

SOME I WRITE
SOME I LOSE IN THE
        MULTIPLE ENTANGLEMENTS
        OF UNCONTROLLED THOUGHTS

THE RIVER IS RUNNING
OVERFLOWING IT'S BANKS
        SO I MUST
        CREATE A DAM

AND YOU SEE IT BEFORE YOUR EYES

        MY DAM FOR MY RIVER
        SLOWING
        LONG ENOUGH TO TRANSFER MY THOUGHTS

SO I MAY RETRIEVE AT WILL OR
LET THE DAM FLOW AT WILL

BUT I MUST REMEMBER
        NOT TO LET THE WATER STAGNATE

THAT'S WHY THE DAM MUST BE OPENED
FROM TIME TO TIME

WOULDN'T IT BE FANTASTIC
IF SOMEONE COULD PLUG
          A COMPUTER IN MY BRAIN
WITH MY PERMISSION OF COURSE
AND RETRIEVE ALL THAT IS
OR HAS BEEN STORED THERE

TOTAL RECALL
BY MODERN SCIENCE

CATAGORY
CATAGORY

THINK HOW AMAZING IT WOULD BE
          TO SEE ALL THAT
                    YOU HAVE SEEN
                    HEARD
                    READ
SINCE BIRTH

AND HOW SAD THE
LACK OF UTILIZATION
THEREOF

YOU MADE ME TRUST

LIKE BLIND FAITH
BUT I GUESS TRUST IS BLIND FAITH

I KNOW YOU WOULD NEVER ALLOW ME
TO BETRAY ME

YOU ALLOW DISCOVERY

I CAN TRUST
I CAN LOVE

HOW NICE
HOW COMFORTABLE

WHY AM IS SO AFRAID TO TOUCH YOU

WHY AM I SO AFRAID TO TELL YOU HOW I FEEL

    IN THIS DAY OF THE LIBERATED WOMAN
    ME THE LIBERATED WOMAN

    AFRAID

BECAUSE I'M NOT SURE YOU'RE A LIBERATED MAN

BECAUSE I'M NOT SURE HOW YOU FEEL
BECAUSE

IF YOU CAN'T ACCEPT
MY LOVE
I CAN'T ACCEPT
LOSING YOUR FRIENDSHIP

    BUT I MAY HAVE TO

YOU TOUCHED MY SOUL
YET YOU NEVER TOUCHED ME

YOU SPEAK SOFTLY
FEEL EVERYTHING DEEPLY

  YOUR EYES
    TENDER
    BRIGHT
    SHINING WITH WONDER
    AS A CHILD'S

YOU DISCOVER LIFE
EVERYDAY

I KNOW YOU WILL NEVER HURT ME
YOU ARE NOT CAPABLE
OF CAUSING
  PAIN

DO YOU KNOW YOUR STRENGTH
YOU ARE THE STRONGEST MAN
  I KNOW

YOU ARE STRONG ENOUGH
  TO CRY

WHO ARE YOU SO FAR AWAY
YOU WHO LOVES ME
WHY THE INFATUATION

YOU MAKE ME FEEL LIKE A TOTAL WOMAN
        WHY YOU ACCEPTED
        MY SAYING NO

YOU WERE MAN ENOUGH
NOT TO FEEL REJECTED

FOR YOU WERE NOT REJECTED
I WANTED MORE THAN PHYSICAL FROM YOU
        AT THE TIME
I WANTED EMOTIONAL
        AS WELL
AND YOU GAVE
AND YOU STILL GIVE

NOW YOU ARE NOT HERE BUT YOU STILL GIVE
AND YOU WILL BE WITH ME FOR A LONG WHILE

THE WARMTH OF YOUR VOICE WHEN YOU CALL
THE MEMORY OF THE WAY YOU TOUCHED
        MY HAND
        MY FACE
WITH SUCH TENDERNESS

YOU CAME BACK LAST NIGHT

WE TALKED OF MY PHILOSOPHIES
AND I LET YOU KNOW
        I WAS NO LONGER IN LOVE WITH YOU

I SAW THE SADNESS IN YOUR EYES
BUT HEARD THE RELIEF IN YOUR VOICE
YOU ARE STILL CONTRADICTING YOURSELF

BUT IT WAS NICE AND COMFORTABLE
TO HAVE YOU HERE AGAIN

        I NEVER LET YOU TALK
        NEXT TIME
        IT'S YOUR TURN

YOU HAVE TAUGHT ME SO MUCH
YOU GAVE
AND CONTINUE
TO GIVE ME SO MUCH

HEY YOU

MISTER
I KNOW YOUR NAME
I KNOW WHERE YOU LIVE

WE HAVE BEEN ACQUAINTANCES FOR SOME TIME

WE HAVE WORKED TOGETHER
WE HAVE PLAYED TOGETHER
I CALL YOU FRIEND

YOU HAVE SEEN ALL MY MOODS
EVEN FEAR
SO FEW HAVE SEEN SO MUCH OF ME

YET I REALLY DON'T KNOW YOU AT ALL
          YOU TALK A LOT
            ABOUT SO MANY THINGS
BUT YOU NEVER TELL ME WHO YOU ARE

OR HAVE YOU
          HAVE I NOT BEEN LISTENING

I PROMISE
I'LL LISTEN A LITTLE CLOSER
          NEXT TIME

MY LANDLORD
WHAT MAKES YOU TICK
MR. MULTIPLE PERSONALITY MAN

      WHY
      YOU KNOW YOU'RE ALWAYS RIGHT

EVEN IN THE LONG RUN
      YET YOU GIVE PEOPLE THEIR LEAD
      THEIR HEAD SO TO SPEAK
      TO RUN AS FREE AND FAST AS POSSIBLE
UNTIL THE REIGNS OF THEIR
OWN FAILURE
SLOWS THEM DOWN

YOU COULD HAVE PUT ME ON THE STREET
MOST WOULD HAVE
BUT I GUESS YOU KNOW I WILL BE FOREVER GRATEFUL
      AND REPAYMENT WILL COME IN TIME

QUICK WIT.....OF COURSE
INTELLIGENT.....OF COURSE
SENSITIVE

I REMEMBER YOU

YOUR EGOTISM
        AND THE DAY YOU SAW
        THE CHILD SLEEPING
        UNDER THE BRIDGE
        AND RECESS WAS OVER
        AND YOU WENT TO FIND HIS TEACHER

YOUR COCKINESS
        THE SUICIDE HOT LINE BY YOUR BED
        THE PAIN YOU FELT FOR OTHERS
        AND THE PEOPLE YOU HELPED TO RESCUE THEMSELVES
        FROM TOTAL DESTRUCTION
        FROM DRUG ADDICTION
        AND IT HURT YOU TO PUNISH TOMMY

YOUR PERFECTIONISM
        A MEDAL FOR YOUR FIRST DOWNHILL RACE
        AND YOU HAD TO WIN AT GIN RUMMY 9 OUT OF 10 HANDS
        YOUR SURE SHOTS AT TARGETS THAT WERE VOID
        OF THEIR BULLSEYES WHEN YOU RAISED YOUR PISTOL

RICK THE TOKEN INDIAN
MIKE THE TOKEN JEW
TOMMY THE TOKEN CHILD
ME THE TOKEN WOMAN
AND YOU THE TOKEN GOD
        A DIRECT QUOTE FROM YOU SIR

I LOVED AND WILL ALWAYS LOVE
OUR TOKEN HOUSEHOLD

AND YOUR TENDERNESS
AND YOUR SMILE
AND OUR LAST GOODBYE

Rick, American, The Astonishment of Belief, Woodcut, 1970

RICK
YOU ARE THE MOST TRUSTING SOUL I HAVE EVER KNOWN
        AT LEAST OF HIS BROTHERS
YOUR PRINT
OF ST. SEBASTIAN
WILL ALWAYS BE IN MY HOME
        "THE ASTONISHMENT OF BELIEF"
I WILL ALWAYS KEEP YOUR PICTURE
I AM PROUD I KNOW YOU

REMEMBER THE NIGHT
JOHNNY CARSON WAS FUNNY
        THE NIGHT YOU SHOT AN IMAGINARY ARROW
        THRU JOHN WAYNE'S HEART
WOUNDED KNEE. . . . .WOUNDED HEART
        LEARNING
        TRAVELING
SO YOU WILL HAVE THE KNOWLEDGE YOU NEED TO
HELP THE SLAVES OF MODERN AMERICA
HOW YOU KNOW YOUR BROTHERS WOULD NOT LET YOU DOWN
WHEN THE DOORS OF WHITE FOUNDATIONS
WERE BEING SLAMMED IN YOUR FACE

.

YOUR WAYS
THE WAY YOU FEEL NEXT TO ME

THE WAY YOU STROKE MY BACK
AND WAKE ME WITH YOUR GENTLE STRENGTH
THE WAY YOU KISS ME
THE WAY YOU HOLD ME
        AFTER WE MAKE LOVE
THE WAY YOU MAKE LOVE TO ME

THE WAY YOU INTERACT AND REACT
WITH MY FRIENDS
AND MY FAMILY
THE WAY YOU PLAY GUITAR
THE WAY YOU CAN'T AND WON'T SING

THE WAY YOU HAVE COFFEE FOR ME
IN THE MORNING
YOU EVEN HAVE A WAY
        WITH CROSSWORD PUZZLES

YOU MUST KNOW
I'M GLAD WE SHARED OUR LIVES

FOR NOW YOU'VE GONE
TOO BAD YOU COULDN'T STAY
BUT THAT'S JUST ANOTHER
WAY OF YOU

AWAY

TODAY I AM TRAVELING
INCOGNITO
ACTUALLY INVISIBLE

SO ONLY THOSE AS INTROSPECTIVE
        AS I
WILL RECOGNIZE ME

I USED TO GO OUT
AND PEOPLE WOULD SEE ME
AND SMILE
AND WAVE
AND TAKE UP MY TIME

AND NOW I GO OUT
AND THOSE THAT SEE ME
APPRECIATE
WHAT I HAVE TO OFFER

AND OTHERS
JUST THINK
A WIND BLEW PAST
THEY ONLY SAW A SHADOW NEAR THEM

AND THEY WILL NEVER KNOW
THAT THEY
MISSED
ME

ARTISTIC CREATIVITY

INSPIRED BY
AN EMOTIONAL REACTION

    TO SOMEONE
    SOMETHING
    SOMEPLACE
    AN EVENT

        FOR ALL OUR YESTERDAYS
        AFFECT OUR TOMORROWS

AND CREATIVITY MUST HAVE AN OUTLET

AND IF AN OUTLET IS NOT FOUND IN THIS LIFE
THEN A FUTURE LIFE

OUR PAST LIFE
HIDDEN IN THE SECRET VALLEY
OUR SOUL
    BUT THERE

AFFECTION OUR ACTION AND REACTION
TO THE EVENTS OF NOW

STRUCTURED LIFE
SCHEDULES
DEADLINES
ALL THOSE PEOPLE TO SEE
ALL THOSE PLACES TO BE
          BUSY
          BUSY
          RUN
          RUN
          HERE
          THERE
          EVERYWHERE
                    STOMACH PAINS
                    HEADACHES
                    NERVOUS TENSION

REMEMBER LEISURE WOODLAND WALKS
AND SIMPLE SMALL TALK
THE SMELL OF WOOD BURNING IN THE FIREPLACE

AND OPEN SPACE
AND NOTHING TO DO
          SO YOU READ
          OR WRITE
          OR PLAY GUITAR
          OR SING A SONG

I'M GOING BACK
WOULD YOU LIKE TO COME ALONG

DO I BELIEVE

IN

REINCARNATION

DO I BELIEVE

IN

GOD

SHALL I ASK YOU A QUESTION

HOW DO YOU LIKE BEING A PAWN
IN A CHESS GAME

BETWEEN

GOD AND BEELZEBUB

A LONG ONE. . . . ACTUALLY THE LONGEST

SITTING IN THE MEMPHIS AIRPORT
WAITING ON ANOTHER DELAYED FLIGHT
ANOTHER FORCED STOP

I WONDER IF IT WEREN'T FOR FORCED STOPS
WOULD I EVER WRITE

THE LAST THIRTY SIX HOURS PACKED WITH THOUGHTS
I HAVE COMMITTED MYSELF AGAIN
                    INTO A STATE OF EXHAUSTION
I KNOW I SHOULD REST
        BUT AGAIN
        I FEEL TIME IS SO SHORT
WITH SO MUCH TO BE ACCOMPLISHED

SO MANY TRAVELERS AROUND ME
        READING
        TALKING
        CHEWING GUM
        SMOKING
ALL ON THEIR WAY
I WONDER OF THEIR INDIVIDUAL DESTINATIONS AND WHY
MINE TO RETURN TO ANOTHER COMMITMENT
THE COMMITMENT OF THAT EIGHT TO FIVE HUM DRUM
AM I BASICALLY LAZY
I THINK NOT
IT'S JUST I ENJOY PEOPLE SO MUCH MORE
        MORE THAN WHAT
WHAT ANALOGY SHALL I MAKKE
        NONE I THINK
IT'S JUST I ENJOY TRADING THOUGHTS WITH OTHERS

I PHILOSOPHIZE
        SELF IS MOST IMPORTANT
        SELF RIGHTS
        SELF WRONGS

A LONG ONE. . . . ACTUALLY THE LONGEST (CONTINUED)

WHY ARE YOU SO GLAD I GOT A JOB
REASONS. . . YOU WANT
I WILL DO IT AND HAVE DONE SO
      BUT
NOT FOR ALL THE REASONS SOME THINK
BUT, FOR MY VERY OWN SELFISH REASONS
      I WILL DO IT SO I CAN ESCAPE AGAIN
      INTO MY WORLD OF REALITY
                OR SOMEONE ELSE'S FANTASY

MY WORLD OF REALITY
WATCHING OTHER RESPOND AND REACT TO ONE ANOTHER
LISTENING TO MUSIC OF MY FRIENDS
      WANTING TO HAVE TIME TO CREATE MY OWN POETRY
      LOOKING AT BUILDINGS AND THEIR CONSTRUCTION
      WANTING TO HAVE FREEDOM TO CREATE MY OWN
      READING THE WORDS MY FRIENDS HAVE WRITTEN
          EVEN THOSE I HAVE NEVER MET
      THINKING OF THOSE THAT ARE PART OF OUR PAST
      AND THINKING ABOUT THE FUTURE OF SOULS
          NOT THE IMMEDIATE FUTURE
          BUT THE UNIVERSAL FUTURE

THE UNIVERSAL FUTURE
      THE UNIVERSAL PAST

GRASP THE THOUGHT OF TOTAL ESCAPISM INTO THE FUTURE
      I PERSONALLY BELIEVE
      I PERSONALLY BELIEVE
      I PERSONALLY BELIEVE

THERE IS NOT ANYTHING IN ANYONE'S IMAGINATION
      THAT IS NOT POSSIBLE
          (I HAVE A WEAKNESS FOR USING NEGATIVES)
EVERYTHING IS POSSIBLE
EVERYTHING IS POSSIBLE
EVERYTHING IS POSSIBLE

A LONG ONE. . . . ACTUALLY THE LONGEST (CONTINUED)

THINK OF THOSE
THAT LAUGHED AT JULES VERN
        LAUGHING SOCIAL JACKELS
        INSANITY
                LAUGH
                LAUGH
                LAUGH

SOME LAUGH AT ME

DID YOU KNOW THEY LOCK UP THOSE PEOPLE
WHO CLAIM TO BE FREDERICK THE GREAT
        OR GEORGE WASHINGTON
        OR ALEXANDER THE GREAT

BUT WHAT IF THEY ARE

WHAT IF THEIR MIND TRANSENDED THE BOUNDARIES
        AND RESTRICTIONS
        OF TIME AND SPACE

SOME SAY IT'S NOT POSSIBLE

        IT'S NOT
                IS IT
                IS IT
                IS IT

BUT, WHAT WOULD YOU SAY IF I TOLD YOU
I BELIEVE IT IS POSSIBLE

WHAT WOULD YOU SAY IF I TOLD YOU
        ANYTHING IS POSSIBLE
                ANYTHING

A LONG ONE. . . . ACTUALLY THE LONGEST (CONTINUED)

YOU SAY YOU BELIEVE
ALL THINGS ARE POSSIBLE
        THROUGH YOUR GOD

BUT, THEN I HEAR YOU SAY THINGS THAT LIMIT
        YOUR GOD

SO, DO YOU REALLY BELIEVE ALL THINGS ARE POSSIBLE

        DO YOU
        DO YOU
        DO YOU
                REALLY

I DO

SOON BACK TO REALITY
OR MY CONSCIENCE REALITY
I CONSIDER IT MY FANTASY
FOR IT IS NOT THE REALITY LIFE
I CHOOSE FOR MYSELF
BUT THE REALITY LIFE I MUST LIVE TO FINANCIALLY
SUPPORT MYSELF

THIS IS WHAT I MUST DO
THIS IS WHAT IS RIGHT

IF YOU DON'T BELIEVE ME JUST ASK SOCIETY
I'M SO GLAD YOU GOT A JOB

WHY CANT I BE INDEPENDENTLY WEALTHY
AND SUPPORT ALL MY ARTISTIC FRIENDS
SO THEY MAY BE FREE TO CREATE

I SOMETIMES
COMPARTMENTALIZE MY THOUGHTS
          MY EMOTIONS

WHEN I CAN'T COPE
          AT THE TIME

THEN BRING THEM OUT
AND DEAL WITH THEM

          ON AN UNEMOTIONAL LEVEL

          SOMETIMES

MY FAN
HANGING
WITH YOUR
        FOUR
WOODEN BLADES
TURNING, TURNING
AM I A BORING ROOMMATE
JUST READING MY BOOKS
AND WRITING ON MY PADS

MY FAN
WHAT CAN YOU TELL ME
WHAT HAVE YOU WITNESSED
IN THIS ROOM OVER THE PAST 50 YEARS

        POLITICAL DEALS
        OIL DEALS
        THE LOVE MAKING OF NEWLYWEDS
        ILLICET SEX. . . . . . CHUCKLE, CHUCKLE
        FIGHTS
        LAUGHTER
        TEARS

MY FAN
AREN'T YOU GLAD ALL YOU HAVE TO DO
        IS TURN AND HUM

MY FAN
I WISH YOU WERE MY FAN
THEN I COULD TAKE YOU HOME WITH ME
        AND I COULD WATCH YOU TURN
        AND LISTEN TO YOU HUM
                HUM
                HUM
                HUM

I HAVE TWO PUPPIES
ONE NAMED SPOOK AND ONE NAMED BLACK LADY
THE OFFSPRING OF MACIE, ONE BEAUTIFUL DALMATION
        AND ONE UNKNOWN ROVER OF THE NIGHT
TO SEE THEIR BLACK COATS SHINING IN THE SUNLIGHT
AS THEY FROLIC WITH MY NEICE JENNIFER
        OR ME
        OR MY PARENTS
MY MOTHER CLAIMS SHE DOESN'T LIKE PETS
SO WHY DOES SHE HAVE OR ALLOW FOUR DOGS RESIDENCE
        MOTHERS THAT IS ANOTHER STORY
LOVE THE WAY THEY PLOP IN MY LAP
        WHEN I SIT IN FRONT OF THE FIRE
LOVE THE WAY THEY SLEEP WITH THEIR HEADS ON ONE ANOTHER
LOVE THE WAY SPOOK PROTECTS LADY
        ALL THE THINGS THEY DO BRING SUCH HAPPINESS

        I HAD TWO PUPPIES
        NOW, BUT ONE

WITH THE FRIENDS I HAVE
AND THE LOVE GENERATED BY THOSE FRIENDS
        I SOMETIMES FORGET
        THAT CRUEL PEOPLE
                        DO EXIST
FOR ONLY AN EMPTY PERSON
        COULD POISON A PUPPY
MY PLAYFUL, LOVING, TRUSTING PUPPY
TRUSTING
PROBABLY LICKED THE HAND THAT FED HIM POISON
IT WOULD HAVE TO BE A STRANGER
FOR SURELY NO ONE THAT HAD SEEN HIS BLACK COAT SHINING
SUNLIT, FROLICKING COULD HAVE DECIDED
        HEY YOU TIME TO DIE

HAVE YOU EVER SEEN A PUPPY WITH A TEAR STAINED FACE
MY BLACK LADY HAS ONE

HELLO

WHAT A NICE SMILE
I'M GLAD

      YOU'RE HERE
      WITH ME
      NOW

JUST BECAUSE YOU'VE BEEN HERE BEFORE

DON'T FORGET

TO LOOK AGAIN
        THERE IS ALWAYS
        MORE THAN ONE PERSPECTIVE

EVEN TO A SINGLE OBJECT

SO EACH TIME YOU PASS

LET
YOUR
UNIVERSE OF SOUL

                DRINK

IN A NEW DROP OF LIQUID
            THOUGHT FOOD

FOR
FUTURE
GROWTH
PATTERNS

INTELLECTUAL
EDUCATED
        JUDGEMENTAL BEINGS

THIS HUMAN RACE OF OURS

HOW CAN INTELLECTUAL
EDUCATED
        BEINGS
        BE JUDGEMENTAL
BY WHOSE STANDARDS
BY WHOSE VESTED POWER

BY OUR OWN
        BUT EACH PERSON
                DIFFERENT
                INDIVIDUAL
WHAT IS RIGHT FOR ONE
MIGHT POSSIBLY BE WRONG FOR ANOTHER
SO WHO IS TO JUDGE

ONLY THAT BEING COMMONLY CALLED GOD
        FOR LACK OF A BETTER WORD
WE ALL HAVE
OUR PERSONAL
OR PRIVATE
        SOME HAVE A PUBLIC GOD

BE IT RELIGIOUS OR NOT

        YOU ARE A JUDGE
                YOU

OF COURSE
I FORGOT
YOU ARE A
        DEMIGOD

WHY DO SO MANY HUMANS HAVE A SAD MISTRUST
OF ANY AND ALL THAT ARE DIFFERENT

WHAT GIVES THEM THEIR SENSE OF SUPERIORITY
        OR INFERIORITY

WHY
WHAT IS
THAT OR THOSE INTANGIBLE THINGS

HOW CAN ONE BEING BE BETTER THAN ANOTHER
        WE ALL HAVE EMOTIONS

                CAN EMOTIONS
                HAVE SHAPES

                        I THINK NOT

CAN WE CHANGE
        AS INDIVIDUALS
        AS GROUPS
FOR SOME CHANGE IS SELDOM
FOR OTHER LIKE THE WIND
        CHANGE CAN BRING
                JOY
                GROWTH
                AT LEAST HOPEFULLY

DO SOME PEOPLE MAKE YOU FEEL
        AS IF YOU ARE BEING CLOSED, OR DROWNED, OR A NET
        DRAWN OVER YOU
THE MORE THEY TALK
        THE TIGHTER THE ROPE BECOMES
        YOU WANT TO SCREAM
YET, YOU MUST REMAIN CALM
        FOR THE MOMENT OF ESCAPE

REACH OUT

FOR BY REACHING OUT
WE CAN BE REACHED

WE HAVE REACHED ONE ANOTHER
IN A WAY
THAT CAN ONLY BE REACHED
        BY THOSE THAT REACH

THANK YOU FOR REACHING ME
AND WHEN WE PASS
ONE ANOTHER
        IN SOME DISTANT FUTURE
INTERFUSED
IN THE OUTER LIMITS
OF THIS UNIVERSE
        OR SOME DISTANT UNIVERSE

TRUST WILL BE
        POSSIBLY INGRAINED
IN OUR MULTIPLE SOULS
        DUE
        TO
        THIS
        ENCOUNTER

SOME PEOPLE KEEP THEIR GARDEN FREE
        OF WEEDS

WHILE STILL OTHERS LET THEM GROW
FINALLY SUFFOCATING
        THE FRUITS
        THE VEGTABLES

SO TO ALL MY FRIENDS
        I SAY
KEEP YOUR LIFE FREE
        OF WEEDS

WEED YOUR GARDEN

LET YOUR TRUE FRIENDS
        ACT AS PLANT FOOD

GROW FREE MY FRIENDS
IN THIS NEW LIFE

TOO BAD
WE ARE NOT ALL THOSE WHO KNOW
FOR THOSE WHO KNOW GENERATE LOVE
        LOVE TO ONE ANOTHER AS WELL AS SELF

BUT ALAS, THE TIME IS NAUGHT
        FOR UTOPIA

UTOPIA
        IS
                KALEIDOSCOPICALLY
                                DRIFTING

SIMPLY
WAITING
SOMEWHERE IN ANOTHER UNIVERSE
        OR ON ANOTHER UNSEEN PLAN

MAYBE SOON
WE WILL ALL BE
        FREE
        FREE
        FREE

AND WE MAY SIMPLY
CLOSE OUR EYES
        AND FLOAT
        WITH OUR NEW FOUND FREEDOM

                FLOAT TO THAT PLANE

ACTUALLY

CONTRADICTION

IS WHAT
PREVENTS IT ALL
FROM BEING BORING

CAN YOU IMAGINE IF NO ONE CONTRADICTED
ANYONE OR ANYTHING

      HARMONY IS ONE THING

BUT
TOTAL
BOREDOM
QUITE ANOTHER

.

THE CAPACITY TO ACCOMPLISH

IS UNLIMITED

ONLY

THE KNOWLEDGE

OF HOW TO
MAKE THE MOST OF OPPORTUNITIES

BUT WHAT DO I REALLY WANT

WHAT AM I SEEKING

LOVE
RESPECT
ADMIRATION

HOW EGOTISTICAL
HOW HUMAN

    WITH FAILURE
    MY GREATEST FEAR

PEOPLE
   THE "I" PEOPLE
   THE "BLAMERS"
   THOSE WHO KNOW

THOSE PEOPLE
ALL OF THOSE PEOPLE
ARE MY HUMAN RACE
   OUR NEEDS DIFFERENT
     YET THE SAME
THE SAME IN THEIR DIFFERENTIALITY
   BURNING OURSELVES TO DEATH
   WITH ENERGY
   WITH TALENT
     UNTIL WE LOVE AND LIVE FOREVER

THE "BLAMERS"
ARE THE "I" PEOPLE WHO CANNOT FACE THEMSELVES
SO THEY BLAME EVERYONE ELSE
FOR ALL THAT IS AT FAULT
WITH THEMSELVES AND THEIR LIVES

THE "I" PEOPLE
CANNOT FACE OTHERS ON A ONE TO ONE BASIS
THEY MUST HAVE THE ATTENTION OF
   ALL AROUND, AT ALL TIMES
NEVER BEING OPEN ENOUGH
   TO ACCEPT LOVE
   BY BEING CLOSED TO LOVE
   THEY OFTEN CREATE HATE
   YET REMAIN TOTALLY UNAWARE OF WHO THEY ARE
     WHAT THEY HAVE CREATED OR WHY

WE ARE ALL "I" PEOPLE
WE ARE ALL "BLAMERS"
WE ARE ALL THOSE WHO KNOW
    WHICH DOMINATES YOU

HEY FACTORY YOU FORGOT A PART
        FOR THIS MACHINE

MAYBE A SWITCH
OR EVEN A PUSH BUTTON
OH, THOSE DAMN MACHINES
THAT HAVE
ENTERED
THE WORLD
OF BUSINESS
MAKE MONEY
SYNDROME
        THEY LOOK HUMAN

THIS HUMAN LOOKING TALKING MACHINE
HAS NO FEELINGS

I KNOW THE FACTORY FORGOT THAT PART WE CALL HEART
THIS MACHINE DOES NOT KNOW OR UNDERSTAND FRIENDSHIP
        OR LOVE
        OR TENDERNESS
                ALL THOSE UNIVERAL LUBRICANTS THAT
                KEEP THE PART CALLED HEART
                WELL OILED

BUT THS ONE DOES NOT
DOES NOT
DOES NOT
DOES NOT
DOES NO
DOES N
DOES
DOE
DO
D

DREAMS
        FLOATING THROUGH THE MIND

        BEAUTY
        TRANQUILITY

PASSING FROM ON LIFE FORM
TO ANOTHER

ALWAYS CHANGING
NEVER STATIONARY
PEOPLE

YOU'VE SEEN
NEVER SEEN
TOUCHED
NEVER TOUCHED
LOVED
NEVER LOVED
PLACES SEEN
NEVER SEEN

DREAMS WHERE REALITY
AND FANTASY MERGE

ALL THINGS POSSIBLE
AT ALL TIMES

THE DISILLUSIONMENT OF IDEALS
THEY CAME TO ME IN A DREAM

MY KNIGHT IN SHINING ARMOUR WAS A VILLIAN
        THE PAIN AS REAL AS REALITY
MY FRIENDSHIP TURNED TO HOMOSEXUAL FANTASY
        THE SHAME AS REAL AS REALITY
MY MINISTER A MONEY STEALING FANATIC
        THE MISTRUST AS REAL AS REALITY
ALL OF THESE THINGS
                HAVE AND CONTINUE TO A PROFOUND EFFECT
                ON ME AND MY THOUGHTS PROCESS AT THIS
TIME
A DREAM SHOULD NOT BE SO REALISTIC
        WHAT IS TRUTH
        AND WHAT DO WE PERCEIVE TRUTH TO BE
        ARE PEOPLE AND THINGS AS WE SEE THEM
        OR WHAT WE WANT TO SEE
                ARE THESE GOOD PEOPLE IN MY LIFE
                REALLY EVIL
                SURELY NOT
                        AM I NOT WHO I THOUGHT
                                ARE YOU NOT YOU
WHAT DOES THIS DREAM SHOW ME
DO DREAMS SHOW TRUTH OR FANTASY. . .OR BOTH
                ARE THEY SUBCONCSCIENCE FEARS
                OR SUBCONSCIENCE REALITY
IF THEY ARE REALITY
THEN ALL I'VE BELIEVED OR PERCEIVED
        WRONG
MY BELIEFS AND PERCEPTIONS ARE A PART OF ME
        THEN AM I WRONG
        IS MY PURPOSE IN LIFE WRONG
                WITHOUT PURPOSE
                I AM NON EXISTANT

I PREFER TO BELIEVE I EXIST

APPREHENSION

I CAN'T SLEEP

      MAYBE FANTASIZE

BUT NO

MY HEAD IS CLOGGED WITH UNDELIVERED
MESSAGES TO MY CONSCIENCE MIND

APPREHENSION

      INTUITION

THE PHONE RINGS

THE FREEDOM OF CHOICE IS UP TO YOU

I WANT TO WRITE
          BUT I CHOOSE NOT TO DO WITHOUT
          CERTAIN MATERIAL POSSESSIONS
                    LUXURIES ONE MIGHT SAY

MUST ONE ALWAYS
          DO WITHOUT
TO DO WHAT THEY WANT
          AS OPPOSED TO WHAT IS EXPECTED
                    AND BY WHOM

WHEN WILL I DO
WHAT I EXPECT

WHY DOES LACK OF ENTHUSIAM
FROM OTHERS
        SLOW MY PROGRESS

I MUST NOT LET OTHERS
HAVE THAT MUCH CONTROL
        OF MY EMOTIONS

GET IT TOGETHER LADY
        YOU DO NOT NEED THE APPROVAL OF OTHERS
TO WRITE THE WORDS WITHIN YOU

REMEMBER
ONLY SOME HAVE SIMILIAR GROWTH PATTERNS
        OTHERS HAVE NO GROWTH PATTERNS
SOME HAVE MORE ACCELERATED GROWTH PATTERNS
SO WHY IN THE WORLD WOULD YOU LET
        THOSE INFLUENCE YOU
                FEAR, MAYBE

THINK OF THOSE THAT SMILE WHEN THEY READ YOUR WORDS
MOST OF THE TIME YOU CAN LAUGH OFF
        THAT SENSE OF REJECTION

IT
IT
IT'S JUST THAT IT'S MORE DIFFICULT
WHEN IT COMES FROM SOMEONE
        YOU RESPECT AND CARE FOR

GUILT
WE ALL LIVE WITH IT OR AT LEAST THOSE
        SENSITIVE TO OTHERS
        HAVE LIVED WITH IT AT ONE TIME OR ANOTHER
WE'VE BEEN TAUGHT BY OUR PARENTAL FIGURES
                RELIGIOUS FIGURES
                POLITICAL FIGURES
                SOCIAL FIGURES
RIGHT AND WRONG
BLACK AND WHITE
        WE REBEL
        EXPERIMENT ON OUR OWN
        TO LEARN
        WHAT IS RIGHT AND WRONG FOR SELF

QUESTIONS ARISE
TO AN EVEN GREATER DEGREE THAN BEFORE
        BECAUSE SOME OF US DISCOVER
        THERE IS NO BLACK AND WHITE EXISTANCE
                THERE ARE SHADES OF GREY

BUT EVEN MORE IMPORTANT
        LIFE ABOUNDS WITH COLOR
                SO SOMETIMES GUILT PERSISTS UNTIL
                THE REALIZATION
GUILT SHOULD BE ON THE SHOULDERS
OF THOSE LIVING IN A LIMITED WORLD
        OF BLACK AND WHITE

HOW SAD
TO BE
        COLOR BLIND

                TO LIFE

WHY ARE THERE SO FEW
THAT REALLY KNOW ME

DO I KEEP ME FROM SO MANY
OR ARE SO MANY BLIND

      DO I PUT BLINDERS ON FOR THEM

OH, BUT THOSE THAT PUT
      ON THEIR GLASSES FOR ME
      A FEW HAVE MAGNIFYING GLASSES

AND ONE OR TWO
MICROSCOPES

THAT
MY FRIENDS
      KEEPS ME GOING

DOUBTS
WE ALL HAVE THEM
        WE DOUBT
                        OUR PURPOSE
                        OUR TALENT
                        OUR LIFE
                        OUR LOVE
                        OUR IDENTITY
                        OUR RELIGION
                        OUR LACK OF ANY OF THE ABOVE

RACKED WITH INSECURITY
RUNNIING IN THE STREETS
I TRY TO TELL YOU
I GUESS IN MY OWN WAY I DOUBT OUR FRIENDSHIP
        FRIENSHIP IS SOMETIMES FRAGILE
                OUR FRIENSHIP IS STRONG, I "THINK"
IF IT BROKEN BY WORDS WELL MEANT, IT WAS NOT FRIENDSHIP
        BUT JUST A PASSING ACQUAINTANCE
YOU RUN FROM ALL YOU KNOW, FROM ME, FROM YOURSELF

YOU ARE PROTECTED BY DISTANCE
WHO ARE YOU RUNNING FROM
WHAT ARE YOU RUNNING FROM
        THAT FEAR. . .IS WITH YOU
        NOT WITH US. . .YOUR FRIENDS
ALL WE HAVE IS LOVE
        WE REACH OUT BUT YOU WITHDRAW
NEVER EXPRESSING TO US OR YOURSELF. . .THE TRUTH

CAN THE TRUTH BE ANYMORE PAINFUL
THAN THOSE UNSPOKEN LIES
YOU USE TO CONCEAL FROM YOURSELF
        WE KNOW
        YOU FEAR
        FEAR

WHEN SOME READ
THE WORDS I WRITE

THEY SEEM
TO KNOW

WHAT I AM TRYING TO SAY
THEY FEEL

      SIMILIAR

THANK YOU FOR SAYING YOU LIKE WHAT I WRITE
      AND THE WAY I WRITE

OH. . . YOU DON'T LIKE SOME

THAT'S OKAY
AT LEAST YOU EXPRESS TO ME
HOW YOU FEEL

I CAN TAKE CRITICISM
IF IT IS CONSTRUCTIVE

AS LONG AS IT IS THE WAY YOU FEEL

      THE REASON I WRITE
      IS TO
      HOPEFULLY
      EVOKE

        EMOTION

Gail and Pam, Madrid, New Mexico, 1997

www.ingramcontent.com/pod-product-compliance
Lightning Source LLC
Chambersburg PA
CBHW072140170626
46813CB00004BA/1627